Soul Cried

Expressions from the Heart!

FIONA PORCH

First Published in 2018
By F.P. Publishing

Copyright © Fiona Porch, 2018

All rights reserved. No part of this book may be reproduced or transmitted in any form or by any means, graphic, electronic, or mechanical, including photocopying, recording, taping or by any information storage retrieval system, without prior written permission from the author, except in the case of brief quotations embodied in critical articles and reviews. The Australian *Copyright Act 1968* (the Act) allows a maximum of one chapter or 10 per cent of this book, whichever is the greater, to be photocopied by any educational institution for its educational purposes provided that the educational institution (or body that administers it) has given a remuneration notice to the Copyright Agency (Australia) under the Act.

Books may be ordered through leading booksellers globally or by contacting: Fiona Porch
www.FionaPorch.com

The author of this book does not dispense medical advice or prescribe the use of any technique as a form of treatment for physical, emotional, or medical problems without the advice of a physician, either directly or indirectly. The intent of the author is only to offer information of a general nature to help you in your quest for emotional and spiritual well-being. In the event you use any of the information in this book for yourself, the author and publisher assume no responsibility for your actions.

Front Cover Image Copyright © Fiona Porch.
Illustrations Copyright © Fiona Porch.

Cataloguing-in-Publication details are available
From the National Library of Australia
www.trove.nla.gov.au

ISBN: 978-0-6482737-2-1 (Paperback)
ISBN: 978-0-6482737-3-8 (E-book)

Contents

Introduction..xi

What Do You See in Me? 1
Lost within Me..3
All I Ask...5
Pull Through...7
Alone in the Dark...9
The View...11
Over the Ocean..13
Next to You...15
Strength..17
Twenty-One Today, Dear Brother......................19
Yours for the Taking..21
Happy Birthday, Dad 23
The Stakes..25
Time...27
For Max..29
What Will Unveil?...31
This Me Is Enough 33
Pondering...35
Your Heart...37
Life without You...39
Worth Waiting For 41
Ready to Fly 43
Find Me..45

No Mountain I Can't Climb..47
Missing You..49
Fall For You..51
That Guiding Light..53
You and Me..55
Make It Through...57
The One...59
Forget 61
Path 63
Stuck Like Glue...65
Just For You...67
Deep Inside..69
One Moment...71
Birthday in Australia 73
Aware 75
Transcend...77
Two Become One..79
Your Star 81
You'll find the Sun..83
Try 85
Eternal Bliss 87
Get Well...89
By My Side..91
Not Meant To Be 93
Be Heard 95
I Am Who I Am 97
It's Me..99
Surrounds Me 101

Why?	103
Love So Strong	105
Get My Ways	107
Something in There	109
Wishing Away	111
On a Road So Long and Far	113
We Will Be	115
I Love You Still	117
Tell Me That You're Mine	119
Where I Stand	121
A Friend	123
Memories of Heartbreak and Lies	125
Who You Are	127
Happen To Me	129
Grow Old with You	131
Moving On	133
Pushing Me Away	135
Play Your Part	137
Fate	139
Me for Me	141
Life	143
Mystery through History	145
Deep within My Heart	147
Got To Be Strong	149
Soul Cried	151
Stand Tall	153
Shoulda Known	155
Memories of You	157

Life without Limits 159
Lessons Learnt 161
Whole 163
Over You 165
Learn To Love Again 167
There's Something 169
Locked Up Inside 171
Every Part of Me 173
Deeper Than the Ocean 175
L.A.X. 177
Dream to Achieve 179
Take Flight 181
Back at the Start 183
So Many Disasters 185
Blue 187
Selfishness and Greed 189
Vow 191
I Dream 193
I've Been 195
Sturdy Steed 197
All That I Am 199

About the Author 201

This book is dedicated to anyone and everyone who has ever struggled through physical or emotional challenges in their life, who maybe never found their outlet to truly express themselves. May you find peace within, through my words of expression in knowing you are not alone...

For me poetry has been my saviour in
keeping my sanity while allowing me to let
all my feelings flow onto the pages...

When I don't share my thoughts in a verbal way,
Poetry is an outlet that lets me have my say...

Introduction

Born in Sydney, Australia on the 12th of July 1982, at the young age of 8 months I was diagnosed with a rare form of dwarfism. So rare that at the time of my birth it was believed I was the only one in Australia with my particular condition. Growing up, I faced many obstacles but continuously aimed to see the positive side of things. With a smile on my face I always endeavour to display my emotions in such a way as to constantly be a positive light to others.

My way of coping came naturally to me during my early teenage years through the discovery of being able to communicate my deepest emotions through poetry. At first it was the only way I knew of, or felt comfortable in letting out my emotions of struggle and pain without ever burdening anyone in my life. Eventually I came to realise that it was such a blessing. As it became a way for me to express various emotions of love and happiness too. Within these poems lies my emotional journey through aspects of my life and act as a vessel for my thoughts and a window into my soul.

I hope that by baring my soul with you all it encourages each and every one of you to know that determination and self belief can push you to achieve amazing things in this life! Allow yourself to feel and relate to the words on these pages in however they may speak to you in your own life experiences. If you would like to get to know more about me and my detailed story leading into these emotions, you can grab a copy of my personal autobiography called "Me, Kniest & Understanding".

What Do You See in Me?

As I walk down the street,
Not knowing who I'll meet,
I see millions of eyes looking at me,
And I'm wondering what they see.

As I enter a shop,
A hundred people stop.
Still wondering why they look
At every step they took.

My legs may not be straight,
But then we're all taught not to hate.
I may not look the same as you,
But then remember: no others do.

So what if I don't look the same?
You're forgetting that I have a brain.
Why does the cruel exterior
Make you dismiss my interior?

By that I mean my heart.
That's where I would start.
I see puzzled faces
In all these different places.

Take the chance
Before you glance.
Don't judge me by what you see.
I'm a person like you, but instead, I'm me!

Lost within Me

I don't know who I am
Or who I want to be.
I want to feel the magic
Flow out and be free.

I want to sing, I want to write,
I want to live and do it right.
I want to laugh; don't want to cry.
So much to do; no time for whys.

I want to dance; I want to fly.
Truly live this life before I die.
Who am I now? Where should I be?
I am feeling so lost within me.

All I Ask

As I look into your eyes,
That's when I realise
You feed my inspiration
Without trepidation.

All it takes is the will to know how.
We will make it through somehow.
There is no doubt inside my mind,
Even though they say love is blind.

We will make it through the rain,
Push through any heartache and pain.
I know a love like ours is hard to find.
All I ask is that to my heart you are kind.

Pull Through

The pain I feel inside
I can no longer hide.
All these years I've tried.
The countless tears I've cried.

I can no longer take
Lying here awake.
This pain I cannot shake
As I feel my body ache.

My soul feels cold and blue.
This much I know is true.
I wish I only knew
How to make myself pull through.

Alone in the Dark

Alone in the dark,
I see a light.
It's calling for me.
I'm losing this fight.
It's pulling me in,
Draining my soul.
I've lost all my will,
And I have no control.

My heart has no home,
No place to rest.
Alone in this room,
I have nothing left.
Nothing to fight for.
No one to care.
All by myself.
My life feels so bare.

But just when I thought
There was nothing I could do,
I felt you around me,
Pulling me through.
And just when I thought
There was nowhere else to go,
Your warmth reassured me.
You gave me hope.

You are my home,
My guiding light,
The force that surrounds me,
And gets me through the night.
You are my shelter
When my world's caving in.
Your spirit provides me
Strength from within.

You are the reason.
You opened my heart.
Now I am no longer
Alone in the dark.

The View

Too many emotions bottled up inside.
Too many tears I have sadly cried.
There are times when it feels like there's nothing I can do
But wish upon a star and hope that dream comes true.

Like a bangle tangled to a chain,
Life can be full of heartache and pain.
I dust myself off and carry on through,
Reach for the stars while I try to enjoy the view.

Over the Ocean

Over the ocean,
Across the sea,
You'll never know
How much you mean to me.

The look in your eyes,
The touch of your skin,
Every time we kiss,
I feel it deep within.

Over the ocean,
Across the sea,
My heart beats so wildly,
Like the wind through the trees.

You are my sun,
My shining light,
My world, my sky,
My stars that guide me through the night.

Over the ocean,
Across the sea.
I wish you were lying
Right next to me.

Next to You

I want to say what's in my heart.
The trouble is, I don't know where to start.
The feelings within, so deep and true,
My heartbeat's pounding just for you.

Sometimes I wish upon the stars
That you were near and not so far.
Over the ocean, past the seas,
I wish that you were here with me.

You always feed my inspiration,
Know how to ease my hesitations.
Even when we're far apart,
You're always here within my heart.

Though you're a million miles away,
I think of you each and every day.
And there's nothing that I won't do
To be right next to you!

Strength

There's strength within our bodies.
There's strength within our minds.
When I think about real, true strength,
There isn't just one basic kind.

The strength that I rely upon
Comes from deep within my heart.
It is my saving grace
When my world seems to fall apart.

No matter how strong my urge could be
To give in and to lose,
I look back and think of all I've overcome,
And I'm reminded of the path I must choose.

Giving up is not an option.
I am grateful in many ways.
For the strength I find within me
Gets me through each and every day.

Twenty-One Today, Dear Brother

My dear brother, I just want you to know
I'm so proud I've gotten to watch you grow.
I have so much love and respect for you.
Your heart is kind, good, pure, and true.

Having you as my brother is so unreal.
Richly blessed is how I truly feel.
So now that you are twenty-one,
Make the most of life, and have some fun.

Yours for the Taking

There's a feeling that you sometimes get,
And you hope it won't turn into regret.
Yet you still decide to risk it all
In the hope that you have made the right call.

You've set yourself up when you already know
The chance could break you or help you grow.
To fall flat on your face is the risk that you take
Or have something amazing truly worth the stakes.

Without risk there can be no reward.
Not taking the chance is something you can't afford.
You can let yourself sink or take a stand.
This life is yours for the taking,
so grab it with both hands.

Happy Birthday, Dad

Today might be your special day,
But you're special to me in every way.
Thank you for always being there for me.
You are the best dad anyone could be.

So let me take this opportunity to say,
As the years go by and we both go grey,
I love you each and every day.
Here's hoping you have a happy birthday!

The Stakes

I sit here alone, inside my own thoughts,
Realising all the heartache I've fought.
Fighting a fight I know I might lose,
Not knowing the path I know I must choose.

Which choice to make?
The least heartache.
My heart could break.
I know the stakes.

There is no right or wrong
As long as I stay strong.
Someday I'm sure I'll know
Just how far I'll go.

The hurt I feel inside
I can no longer hide.
I know that I must set myself free.
And the only way I can is to just be me.

Time

Waiting for the clock to turn,
Waiting for the time to burn.
Trying hard to contain myself
As the clock ticks slowly on the shelf.

Decisions here, decisions there.
What can I live with when nothing seems fair?
It's hard to be strong all the time.
The pressures can mount higher than what I can climb.

Time is precious, not to be rushed.
Emotions are important, not to be hushed.
I must allow myself the time I need to feel.
Take a step back, and let my soul heal.

When I feel as though I can't go on,
I'll try to hold my head high; I know I am strong.
Because just as time moves into the past,
I will rise above it all, and those troubles won't last.

As I sit in my room, feeling tired and cold,
Time passes so quickly; it's time to be bold.
So much to do; it's now or never.
No time to waste; we don't have forever.

For Max

(14th November 2016)

My heart is sad and lonely.
I didn't want to say goodbye.
As you quietly slipped away,
All I could do was cry.

You will never be forgotten.
I've loved you from the start.
And I'll always keep the paw prints
You left imprinted on my heart.

I love you, Max! xoxo

What Will Unveil?

There is so much that I'd love to share,
But open my mouth, I do not dare.
Emotions are flowing like the wind in the trees
As I take a deep breath and endeavour to breathe.

I've taken a chance and knocked on the door,
Not knowing whether the outcome
will knock me to the floor.
Expecting the worst as I risk the call,
But praying deep down that it's worth it all.

As I nervously wait for the time to pass,
I pray my hope isn't shattered into pieces of glass.
Alone in my thoughts, confused and frail,
As I wait to see what outcome will unveil.

This Me Is Enough

When I was younger,
I couldn't deal.
People kept telling me
Just how I should feel.

I kept my head down,
My feelings inside,
Felt so alone;
Sometimes, I wanted to hide.

But now I know
To hold my head high,
Soar like a bird,
Flying through the sky.

Sometimes life gives you
A chance to see
That things in this world
Are exactly how they should be.

I am who I am;
I have always been tough.
It's time that I shine
'Cause this me is enough.

Pondering...

As I sit here pondering; on all that I feel.
I can't help but wonder; what's fake and what's real.
Emotions are flowing as deep as the sea.
I wish I could explain what's happening to me.

I'm feeling alone, with no place to go.
But deep down I know this really isn't so.
I know that someone is out there somewhere.
Willing, and waiting, and wanting to care.

Wishing and hoping is all I can do.
That things; will work out, and I'll learn what's true.
If I open my eyes, and open my heart.
Then maybe I'll learn, and I'll know where to start.

Your Heart

When your world falls apart.
And you don't know where to start.
Just try to find the answer.
It's buried deep inside your heart.

Life without You

I woke up one morning and I knew.
I realised my heart was so blue.
I didn't want to hear it,
But my head began to fear it.
For what is my life without you?

Worth Waiting For

There is so much I would love to say.
You took my sadness and blues away.
You opened my heart to love again.
When I thought that it would never mend.

When I see you smiling back at me.
You open my soul and set it free.
Your eyes are the window right into your heart.
Special and rare like a work of art.

Never have I met someone like you.
That makes me feel the way you do.
That picks me up when I feel down.
Someone who'll always be around.

I have never felt this way before.
You leave me always wanting more.
I thought I knew what love was before,
But now I know, this love was worth waiting for.

Ready to Fly

When I lost all my hope
You were my light in the dark.
You unlocked my soul
You're the key to my heart.

You're the wind in my sails.
And the stars in my sky.
Your love lifts me up,
Now I'm ready to fly.

Find Me

I'm feeling lost.
I feel afraid.
I'm looking for that star
That's floating far away.

Who am I now?
Where should I be?
I'm feeling all alone
I'm searching too, are you?

But I manage to stay lost.
Kept drowning in the sea,
Not knowing who I was.
Until, you came to find me.

No Mountain I Can't Climb

As time is passing
My mind begins to run.
But I really don't know
What have I become?

Searching deep within,
Into the depths of my soul,
I feel my spirit calling,
I'm about to lose control.

An answer, I am waiting.
Goosebumps tickle my skin.
Emotions overwhelm me,
I want to let you in.

I take a deep breath
There's a whisper in my ear.
As I begin to realise,
There is nothing left to fear.

All worries subside
As I feel frozen in time,
I feel warmth surround me.
There is no mountain I can't climb.

Missing You

There is something that I want to say,
I miss your smile each and every day.
I want to make you happy as best as I can.
Make you smile each moment is my only plan.

When I think of you it's like I'm in a dream.
'Cause baby you make me feel like a beauty queen.
If only you knew, how special you are to me.
When I wake up each day, it's you I want to see.

I can't wait to hold you and feel your touch.
Be with you each day, I miss you so much.

Fall For You

You may be far yet you are near,
'Cause in my heart I hold you dear.
I think about you day and night.
I long to feel you hold me tight.
You stole a place inside my heart.
We were connected right from the start.
I only hope you feel it too,
'Cause I couldn't help but fall for you.

I thought I'd never feel this way,
But it's getting stronger every day.
It's hard not to let my feelings show,
The more I learn about you, the more they grow.
We've both been hurt throughout our past,
But now I want you; to be my last.
I really hope you feel this too.
'Cause I couldn't help but fall for you.

When everything is said and done.
My heart is screaming you're the one.
I've never known someone like you,
It's like you're too good to be true.
I feel like I've known you all along,
I've never felt something so strong.
I truly hope you feel it too,
'Cause I couldn't help but fall for you.

That Guiding Light

Sometimes in this life, we only get one moment to shine.
So grab it with both hands and don't waste any time.
Things are sent to try you,
Push you and define you.
You've got to let your spirit soar and shine so bright.
You know that you can be that guiding light.

Sometimes when we fall, it sets us up
to feel like we can't go on.
But that's when you have got to hold on and be strong.
Things are sent to try you,
Push you and define you.
The world is at your feet,
Don't let it get you beat.
You've got to let your spirit soar and shine so bright.
You know that you can be that guiding light.

You and Me

If love was a bird
I have lost all my wings.
If love is a voice
I can no longer sing.

If love is a house
It's no longer my home.
If love is the sea
It has turned into stone.

The river runs free
Like the shore to the sea.
But love is not love,
'Cause it's gone for you and me.

Make It Through

When you feel lost and afraid and you can't find your way,
Not knowing what to do or how to say
the things you need to say.
You just keep pushing on,
Even though the road seems long.
You can make it through the night,
As long as you don't give up the fight.

The hurt and the pain,
Sometimes drives you insane.
You have everything to lose, and yet so much to gain.
That's when you feel like your life is in vain.
You will make it through the night,
Just don't give up the fight.

The One

When your heart is trapped by the stars in his eyes,
When you'd walk on the moon just to make him realise,
For the feelings that you have locked deep inside,
And you no longer have the will to control or hide.

When you know how you feel but you don't understand,
When your whole body freezes by the touch of his hand,
For the love that you have shines brighter than the sun,
That's when you know you have truly found the one.

Forget

When your heart is filled with shadows,
Feeling pierced with many arrows,
And the sun begins to set,
As you try to forget.

Path

When all the chips fall to the ground,
Who can you count on to be around?
When emptiness has stole your heart,
Look deep inside to find your path.

Stuck Like Glue

Like the feeling you get from your toes in the sand.
Being with you is like being in wonderland.

You bring out so many emotions I never thought I'd feel.
Sometimes I have to pinch myself to know that this is real.

I'm emotionally hooked on you,
It's like I bounce off of you, yet we're stuck like glue.

Just For You

If only I could show you, how much I love you so.
If only I could hold you, my love forever grows.
You've always had a place, right inside my heart.
These feelings have been there, even from the very start.

I've tried so hard to let you know,
That I truly don't know how, to let you go.
I know that we both did wrong,
But I can't stay mad, at you for long.

Please, can we both forgive the past?
Because the love we shared I believe is meant to last.
I'm struggling to give you space.
Please don't dismiss me in haste?

You know when you need me I'm always there.
So can you please just let our hearts repair?
I wrote this poem just for you.
Please realise that what we have is true.

I'm sorry if I handled things all wrong.
Can we make things right? I know our love is strong.
Please don't be mad at me, for loving you so.
Please forgive me and don't let me go.

Deep Inside

I feel dead
Deep inside,
Nowhere to run,
Nowhere to hide,
I wish I may
I wish I might,
Erase these feelings
I feel tonight.
With all the pain
Deep inside,
I'd fake a smile,
But I can't hide.
I'd fake a laugh,
With pain inside,
I'd tell the truth
You'll think I've lied.
Nowhere to run,
Nowhere to hide,
The pain I've felt
The tears I've cried.
That is how I feel
Deep inside!

One Moment

If you only had one moment
To let your feelings show.
Take an opportunity
And really let me know.

Birthday in Australia

Welcome to the Aussie coast.
Where people eat vegemite on toast,
Where thongs are worn on your feet,
And lamingtons are an Aussie treat.

This year as you ventured over land and sea,
I'm glad that you get to spend your birthday with me.
As I try to find the words to say,
I hope you enjoy your special day.

Aware

(Dwarfism Awareness Month October)

There is something that I'd like to share,
For all the people who aren't aware.
This month is especially important to me,
And for the whole dwarfism community.

Kniest, Achondroplasia and SED,
There are over 200 types in the world you see.
We are all human and we all have dreams.
Each of us is different, it all comes down to our Genes.

There are many things that define us, aside from height.
So hopefully this poem will shed some light.
I may be shorter, you may be tall.
I'd like to be called by my name, above all.

If you have a question, it's better to ask.
Now doesn't that sound; like a simple enough task?
Everyone matters, and has a right to be heard.
So please help create awareness, and spread the word.

Transcend

Sometimes when I try and lay my head to rest
My brain won't shut off,
and my thoughts need to be expressed.
There are things that I would love to share,
But blurting them out I just wouldn't dare.

We must live for the moment, and not in the past.
Cherish the memories, make them last.
Yet as another year passes and comes to an end.
Let past lessons guide you, and to greatness transcend!

Two Become One

The beauty within, is like the wind kissing the trees.
Love can grow so sweetly, like honey from the bees.
A heart that's warm and tender, is all I'd ever need.
To fill my life with laughter, without selfishness or greed,
If you're looking for perfection,
see the reflection in my eyes.
Sometimes it's right in front of you, hoping you'll realise.

A person's love can be as deep as the deep blue sky.
Waiting for acceptance so I can spread my wings and fly,
Beauty from within shines brighter than the sun,
Let two hearts melt together and two become one.

Your Star

The reality when you spend so much time
caring about not hurting someone else's feelings
that you end up getting hurt by them.
(So the best thing to do is...)

When you grab the moon and stars,
Not to let them see your scars.
Embrace the changes life sends your way,
Keep moving forward tomorrow's a new day.
Be the positive light you know you are,
Then you'll have them wishing they caught your star.

You'll find the Sun

When the road gets too rough
And it all seems too much.
Remember the world's at your feet.
You must pick yourself up
No matter how tough.
Never facing defeat!

I know it's easier said than done.
Remember, behind each storm shines the sun.
Each battle fought, is a battle won.
If you keep moving, you'll find the sun.

With every mistake; is a new lesson learnt.
Every heartache; is yet another bridge burned.
The choices we make, can lead us astray,
But if you keep moving, you'll find your way.

Yes, I know it's easier said than done,
Remember, behind each storm shines the sun.
Each battle fought, is a battle won.
If you keep moving, you'll find the sun.

Try

As long as you try,
Don't stop to ask why,
Just reach for the sky,
No matter how high.

Eternal Bliss

Sometimes you feel a certain way,
But you don't know the right words to say.
Exactly how it is that you feel,
Though his heart is all, you want to steal.

All it takes is just one look.
To know he's got you hooked.
In the depth of his gaze,
Knowing your heart is trapped in his maze.

Sometimes the words that are unspoken
Can leave you feeling the most heartbroken,
As an opportunity slips past,
And a memory is all that lasts.

If you could just have one more chance,
You'd stay forever locked in his glance.
Take the opportunity that you missed,
Just hold him close to stay forever in eternal bliss.

Get Well

I wish I had a magic wand,
To make it go away.
I'd wave my wand over you,
And make you feel okay.

My thoughts and love are with you,
To stop you feeling blue,
If only I could cast a spell.
I'd simply wish that you are well.

By My Side

I love you
More than you know,
And I want to
Really let it show.
'Cause you make me
Feel so alive,
And I know that with
You by my side, I will survive.

Not Meant To Be

Some of the things that you said,
Just keep going around inside my head.
You can't tell me that you want to be,
The one that goes home with me.

There is so much to gain, yet so much to lose.
We are both to blame, for the path we didn't choose.
Even if we were on the same page,
or even in the same book.
The reality of who we are can't be overlooked.

After all these years, it doesn't make sense.
Our ups and downs were always intense.
I love you just as much as I know you love me,
But something inside, tells me it's not meant to be.

Be Heard

I've lost my focus.
I've lost my way.
I'm going through the motions,
But it's just another day.

It's like I've stopped turning the pages
And I'm stuck on the same word.
I need to find my way out
And let my art be heard.

I Am Who I Am

As I lay on my bed and stare at the ceiling.
I find out all the emotions that I'm feeling.
Frightened, afraid, of what I may find.
Floating visions; in my mind.

Visions of people laughing and staring,
I can't take all this pain that I'm bearing.
Why are they laughing? Is it what they see?
I guess they think they're better than me.

Guy's think you're not even good enough to get to know,
So they take one look and decide to go.
I guess they don't know that real beauty
comes from inside.
Maybe they might learn, if they even bothered or tried.
They think if you're pretty they'll have it all,
But yet they don't realise they're about to fall.

Girls are the same.
You're always to blame.
You'll never be good enough to fit in their gang.
They're always ready to blow you up with a bang.

Why are people like that? I guess I can't really say.
I do know that they want everything their own way.
I always wished and hoped that I was more pretty,
I used to sit and cry and get real shitty.

If you tried to open your mind and see,
You would find out, what a nice person
you'd see inside of me.
I can guarantee, that I'm human and a person too,
So treat me the way you'd want me to treat you.

One day I wish it would go my own way,
But unlikely to happen, in this world I must pray.
That things will work out if I trust and believe.
There is no limit, to what I can achieve.

One day I hope to be seen like a person with a name.
Like "Oh, there goes Jackie, Rachel or Sam"...
Well "Hi, my names Fiona, and I am who I am!"

It's Me

Every morning I wake up it's another day gone by,
But with no one to help me I sit and wonder why?
Why was I brought into a life full of strain?
Heartache and loneliness, to a life full of pain.

I often wished that I wasn't alive.
To this world I wished I didn't arrive.
If you asked me; why I look so sad,
My answer would be; my whole life was bad.

I sit here and cry, with no place to go.
No one to see, my only friend in this world is me.
One question I ask? No answer I see,
But a lonely picture of a girl, it's me!

Surrounds Me

The beautiful skies,
The flowing sea,
The glow in their eyes,
And the wind in the trees,
That's what I see,
That surrounds me.

Why?

Why do I feel the way I do?
Why can't I just stop loving you?
Why is the only question I ask?
Why is the future as bad as the past?

Why is the only thing I want to know?
Why can't I just let you go?
Why I guess I'll never know?
Why because you never let it show!

Why do I ask why?
Why don't I just die?
Why do I sit here and cry?
Why, because I love this guy!

Why do I love this guy so much?
Why do I shiver every time we touch?
Why is the question that I have to ask?
Why can't you answer this simple task?

Love So Strong

I have all this love in my heart
I know that it's all for you.
If only my words could show you,
How deep, my love is and how true.

My heart has been closed up for so many years,
Until you came along; and emptied all my fears.
The love I feel is so strong.
That's how I know we both belong.

I know you feel the same way; I see it written in your eyes.
And I know that our love will always stay alive.

You hold the key to open up the door,
And together we will be for sure.
The love I feel is so strong.
That's how I know we both belong.

I'll be there when the road is rough
and everything goes wrong.
Don't worry 'cause our love is strong.

All I ask is for your love in return,
'Cause without your love, I know
that I'll just crash and burn.
But together we will be one day.
And together we will fly away.
Through the good times; and the bad,
The fun times; and the sad...

Spirit to Spirit, Heart to Heart,
I know our love will never part.
'Cause the love I feel is so strong.
That's how I know we both belong.

Get My Ways

I think of you when I wake up.
I see you in my coffee cup.
I see you when I get to school.
You look so hot, but act so cool.

I see you wherever I go,
But you act like you don't know.
Why can't you say you love me too?
Then I won't have to be so blue.

My friends say that you do, but you say you don't.
I ask you to tell me, but you say you won't.
I love you the most in every way.
I just hope you love me back someday.

I'm obsessed, now I'm depressed.
I wish I was as pretty as the rest.
I love you always; I could say this for days.
I'd do anything to get my ways.

Something in There

Today I found out something,
That I've been waiting to hear for a very long time.
You told me I was worth a dime.
You told me you liked me, I was head over heels.
I could have been spinning, if I had a set of wheels.

But then you said I'm too old for you.
That really broke my heart in two.
Give me a chance, let us try.
Even if I end up, having to cry.

I want it to work, I really do.
I'd do what it is you want me to.
Please tell me you will.
Don't give me the drill.

At first I thought you didn't care,
But now I know you have something in there.

Wishing Away

There are times in life when the road is rough
And everything goes wrong.
Everything you say and do
Can be said in a single; little song.

Sometimes I wish upon a star
That I wasn't here, but very far,
Out of this world is where I should be.
Why, because there's nothing here for me.

Some people try to tell me
Just be happy with what you've got,
But with all the things going through my head
It's not a simple plot.

There are people that I love so much,
But can't get close enough to touch.
When I try to say what's really in my heart,
I feel myself getting hit with the sharpest dart.

I try to keep things to myself,
through days and things I do,
But as the days go by all I see is blue.
Blue, because it frees my heart; when I see the big blue sky.
Wishing and hoping when it will be my turn to fly.

On a Road So Long and Far

As I sit in the car
On a road so long and far,
With you by my side, dear,
I have nothing to fear.

The radio on; with songs I've never heard.
As I look outside, I see a flying bird.
My brother on the other side of me
So young and free, not knowing what his life is yet to be.

My mum in the driver's seat,
Moving the pedals; with her feet.
My dad next to my mum
I know this poem to you might sound dumb.

As I sit in the car
On a road so long and far,
On an outing with the ones I love.
I thank the lord from up above.

We Will Be

You're the only thing racing through my head
As I'm lying here on my bed,
Wishing you were here right now, and by my side forever.
That's the way it should be, just you and me together.

I know you feel the same,
Neither one of us is to blame.
I know we'll be together over time,
Then we will both really shine.

Always full of love you and me,
Together, forever we will be.

I Love You Still

Every time I see your face
You are staring into space.
What are you looking at? I can't see.
Are you looking at her? or looking at me?

I thought of asking you out one day,
But I'm not real sure if you feel that way.
I'm not real sure if it's right.
I'm still not sure if I might.

I cannot talk to you, I'd rather not.
I just wish, it could be forgot.
I'll always love you, I know I will.
Whatever happens, I love you still.

But just as I was about to ask,
I felt like I was smashed into glass.
When I found out it wasn't me.
It was my best friend to be.

Please tell me now just how you feel.
I know whatever happens, I'll love you still.

Tell Me That You're Mine

I will always hold you close to me,
As I look into your eyes, you're all I see.
All the moments that I share with you,
It's all I want to do; it's all I want to do.

My heart is in your hands.
My love forever stands.
Holding you tighter each day,
Together we will stay.

Let me be the one who shares this world.
I'll do anything, to be your girl.
We'll share it together you and I.
Soar like the birds in the sky.

I will show you the world tonight.
We'll see the stars shining bright.
The sparkle in your eyes; sure does shine.
Please, won't you tell me that you're mine?

Where I Stand

Where, where, where do I stand?
Are you going to take my hand?
Are you going to be my man?
Nothing seems to be going to plan.

When I see you looking at me,
Something in your heart feels lost at sea.
It feels like your love for me is dying,
Can't you see, deep within my heart is crying?

Please, can't you stop all of this hurt?
I feel like I've been pushed in the dirt.
Not knowing for sure makes it all worse,
I feel as though I'm stuck in the wicked witches' curse.

If you never speak the truth from inside your heart,
How will I ever know, is it better to part?
Please tell me if this is what you planned?
I need to know where I stand.

A Friend

You need a friend to talk to,
To tell them all your dreams,
Someone you can rely on
When things fall at the seams.

Someone you really trust,
Someone who really cares,
Someone who respects you
And shows you that they're there.

In life you need a friend
To take away your loneliness and sorrow,
With a friend by your side
You'll share a brighter tomorrow.

Memories of Heartbreak and Lies

When I look into the corners of my heart
My heart begins to yearn.
Why does this keep happening to me?
Will I ever learn?

As I look around and see the memories
In each and every room,
All that I'm reminded of
Is the sadness and gloom.

A pool of tears are getting ready
And are filling up around my eyes,
At the end, all I have are these memories
Filled with heartbreak and lies.

Who You Are

Living without risks is like not living at all,
Your heart is never open
because you're afraid you might fall.
Pretending you are someone else,
will not get you far.
Allow yourself to be true inside and out
See the beauty in who you are.

When you feel like you can't go on,
just reach out for my hand.
Remember not to be afraid
and keep telling yourself you can.
Each person is born different
each one of us is a shining star,
Be honest kind and true, but most of all
embrace who you are.

Happen To Me

Just when I thought my life couldn't change,
You walked right in and now my life has rearranged.
You opened your heart and gave me the key,
I never thought that this could happen to me.

You walk in the room and nothing feels the same,
One look in your eyes and my heart feels no pain.
You whisper in my ear; everything will be okay,
I never imagined anything happening this way.
All these emotions and feelings send shivers right through,
I never thought this would happen with you.

I always thought you were out of my league,
Before I had met you, my heart felt fatigued.
I know this is how a love should be,
But I never thought this would happen to me.

Grow Old with You

I woke up
To a brand new day,
The sun was shining
I feel happy in every way.

Your Smiling glow
The spark in your eyes,
The truth in your face
Tells me no lies.

I hope this lasts forever
Forever we will be,
Together in this world
Is a life for you and me.

My life feels so much brighter
Brighter than the sun,
Since you came in
You livened it up with fun.

As long as we're together
I know we'll never be blue,
I know it deep within my bones
I want to grow old with you.

Moving On

I've got to move on.
You've got to get out,
'Cause every time I open up my door
You make me scream and shout.
I can't take no more
I hate all these fights,
Every time I tell the truth
It doesn't come out right.

Why do I have to go through?
All of this pain.
Why am I the one?
Always left to carry the blame
I tell myself, I've got to hold on
I've got to believe.
If it's ever going to work
I can't just up and leave.

Why does it hurt?
I'm fighting back the tears.
After everything we've been through,
Did we both waste all these years?
I've got to stay true,
I've got to stand tall and strong,
If moving on is the only answer
It hurts to accept we don't belong.

Pushing Me Away

Don't know what to do
Don't know what to say,
Every time I come running to you
You keep pushing me away.

Where do I go?
Who do I see?
No one else in this place
But you for me.

I find it hard to tell you
What my heart feels deep inside,
So I open myself up
There's nowhere left to hide.

But now the tears are flowing
Guess there's no more I can say,
It's like I wasted all my love on you
'Cause you just keep pushing me away.

Play Your Part

Just thinking to myself...
How much I have fought to be where I am today,
The endless stories I could tell you,
And all the roadblocks that came my way.
It hasn't been without struggle, right from the very start,
But no matter what life threw my way
I fought with all my heart.

This world is like a rollercoaster; full of endless emotions.
We only ever get to where we want to be
With sacrifice and devotion.
Good or bad,
Happy or sad.

They say what's meant to be will be,
Find what makes you happy and set your spirit free.
Wherever the road takes you, it's only just the start.
Remember, life is what you make it,
but you have to play your part.

Fate

I have a love for you that's too strong for me to hide,
I am going to start by telling you what it is I feel inside.
I hope my feelings don't scare you and you feel it too,
You mean more to me than anything, I have to be true.

I pray that this doesn't all go wrong,
I've waited to say these words to you for so long.
They say good things come to those who wait,
I've waited long enough, now it's time
to take a chance on fate.

Me for Me

Sometimes I feel so alone,
Like the world has given up on me.
I try so hard to hold my head high,
Be positive as much as I can be.

All I want is to feel accepted.
To know that I belong,
But people can be so hurtful,
They don't see how hard it is to stay strong.

I wish that people could see
The me that's inside.
The one who keeps fighting
Even when I may want to hide.

Sometimes people make me question
If it's even worth a shot,
To fight for my dreams
And give it all I've got.

Please just accept me for me
Are the words I want to say,
Because no matter how you challenge me
I'll keep on fighting every day.

Life

Sometimes life can throw you off the rails,
And sometimes it takes you on many different trails.
Life will always take you places that are new.
It even takes you back in time to when things were blue.

See the fire in your eyes and let your dreams burn bright.
See the glitter and glow like the stars shimmering at night.
Let their light show you the way,
Remember this life is yours so cherish every day.

And when the day seems dark and lonely,
look up to the stars,
Stop focusing on the negative,
stop hiding behind life's scars.
Don't let your pain consume you,
and cut you like a knife,
Let all your worries float away,
and your dreams come to life.

Mystery through History

Life is full of mystery,
It changes throughout history.
No matter where you look,
Each day is an unopened book.
Not knowing what will happen next.
Until you flip the page and read the text.

Deep within My Heart

(Dedicated to my Uncle Joe)

When I look outside my window
And all I see is dark,
But I know that you're in heaven
I feel it deep within my heart.

You were so happy and so spirited
Never let things get you down,
And that's the way you'll be remembered,
But the pain will always be around.

You were like an angel.
Sent to us on borrowed time,
I feel graced to have known you
And the mountains we do climb.

To lose someone you love.
The sorrow hurts so much.
I wish that I could see you,
But you're too far to touch.

You know that you are loved always,
And you know you'll be in our hearts every day.
I don't want to be this sad anymore,
I miss you more than I can say,
Each and every day!

Got To Be Strong

When everything around me,
Just seems to fall apart.
I don't know where I'm going,
And I don't know where to start.

If I only had some answers.
To know what I have to do.
If I could understand the reasons,
Why I feel so blue.

Sometimes I sit and wonder
Will I ever belong?
I just want to express my feelings,
So I'm writing this song.

I believe there is a purpose,
For doing what we do,
But when no one understands me
How do I get through?

So I've got to be strong.
I've got to have faith.
I've got to keep moving on
In this time and place.

Soul Cried

There's nothing small about my ambition.
All I want is for people to give me a shot and listen.
I've poured my heart and soul onto these pages,
Through my life, love, and loss, the many different stages.

I've expressed my emotions from deep within,
Sometimes it's been hard to continue to grin.
My soul cried out as I wrote each word,
But now I know it's my moment
and I'm ready to be heard.

Stand Tall

Anything is possible
If you just believe.
Look inside your heart.
Don't give up or just leave.

Open up your eyes
Believe in who you are.
In each and every one of us
There is a shining star.

Break down all the boundaries.
Push through all the walls.
Have faith in yourself,
And rise from each fall.

Things are sent to try us
Make us feel so small.
Push us to the limit,
Don't give up just stand tall.

Shoulda Known

I feel the thunder, I feel the pain.
My heart is yearning, and calling out your name.
I tried to tell you, how I feel.
It's never easy, to hear what's real.

You shut me out, and threw away the key.
I feel so blind, 'cause the truth I didn't see.
You said you loved me, and then you still broke my heart.
I saw the signs, but ignored them from the start.

I was a fool, thinking that you might change.
I never knew, because you kept me out of range.
You broke my heart, with the words you didn't say.
I shoulda known better, than to let you hurt me this way.

Memories of You

No matter what I do
Or how hard I try,
You were a part of me
That I can't deny.
The memories of you
Are etched in my mind,
Why can't I forget?
And leave it all behind.

I shared my life with you
The good times and bad,
It hurts sometimes to think
That's all we ever had.
You broke my heart in two
With each and every lie,
The words you never spoke
And the tears you made me cry.

I ask myself
Time and time again,
Why'd he have to leave?
I lost my best friend.
I ask myself
Each and every day,
Was there something I could do?
That would have made him stay.

But the memories of you
Are etched in my mind,
Why can't I forget?
And leave it all behind.

Life without Limits

When people try to bring you down,
Just get up and don't look back.
Don't let them push you around,
Reach for the stars and stay on track.

Trust with all your heart and soul,
Nothing comes to those who wait.
Live your dreams pursue your goals,
Believe in you and just have faith.

Fight with every part of you,
You have the strength now let it show.
You can make your dreams come true,
Hold your head high and don't let go.

I want to live a life without limits,
Be all I can be.
Show the world I can do it,
There's nothing stopping me.

Lessons Learnt

If you fall don't be afraid
You have the will, now just be brave.
Life is full of twists and turns,
Battles fought and lessons learnt.

Whole

The sunshine to my day
Has brightened up my soul,
The moon of my night,
Has made me feel whole.

Over You

You tried to hurt me with your lies
Instead, you made me stronger.
Just like all the other guys,
I won't put up with this no longer.

At first I thought you were the one
Who'd hold my hand, but now I'm done.
I gave my heart and soul to you,
Like all the rest you were untrue.

I thought that you'd always be mine,
But you were just a waste of time.
I pity the fool who trusts you next,
Never gets your heart or your respect.

Don't feel sorry for me, I know the truth.
I'm happy that we're through.
Let me tell you now, you're not worth the pain,
I'm finally over you.

Learn To Love Again

I'm feeling lost within me, I don't know where to start.
I'm searching for that moment, deep inside my heart.
You left me cold and lonely,
when you walked out my door.
Sitting here in silence, my tears flowing to the floor.

I see the world around me, crumble to the ground.
I feel the noise surround me, but I can't hear a sound.
Sometimes I wish you never left, you tore me apart.
I need to pick myself back up, rewind and restart.

I want to forget, set my heart free.
I cried so hard that I couldn't see.
I'm on my own, I feel afraid.
As I lay here alone where we once laid.

I need to learn to love again
Let go of the hurt and pain,
Break free from your memories
Rise above and feel no shame.

I want to laugh, don't want to cry.
You scarred me when you said goodbye.
Everything I thought I knew
Stopped making sense when I lost you.

There's Something

There's something about the way you make me feel,
One look in your eyes turns my body to steel.
My emotions are flowing as deep as the sea,
One touch from you makes me quiver
Like the wind through the trees.

There's something about you, I can't even explain,
I don't want to move, you release all my pain.
When I'm with you, I feel a magic inside,
It's like you run through my veins, I can't run and hide.

Locked Up Inside

The hurt and the pain used to drive me insane
To the point that I cried myself to sleep,
When the road seemed too rough, I just picked myself up
No one knowing the secrets I would keep.

But I kept it all locked up inside.
Put a smile on my face and my tears I would hide.
Yes, I kept it all deep in my heart,
Like a light switch went off and inside I was dark.

Every Part of Me

I travelled the world.
I searched my heart.
I knew it was you
Right from the start.

You opened the door.
Made me feel whole,
I gave myself to you
Heart, body and soul.

I tried to make a difference.
I was the lock you were the key.
You broke down all my hinges,
Destroyed every part of me.

Deeper Than the Ocean

My heart is like a waterfall.
Flowing with emotion,
The love that I once felt for you
Is buried deeper than the ocean.

L.A.X.

Sitting here at L.A.X.
Thinking about what is next.
My heart is full, yet empty too,
My mind is already missing you.

Waiting here to board my plane,
All the memories are flowing through my brain.
I cherish you all with all my heart.
Leaving is always the hardest part.

I couldn't even begin to explain,
That I'm already waiting to see you again.
You may be far, but in my heart you're near.
'Till I see you again, I'll continue to hold you dear.

Dream to Achieve

There are times when I wake up and it's hard to believe,
All the things in life that I dream to achieve.
I have always known what I want, this is true,
But making it happen is a hard thing to do.

Take Flight

Sometimes I just want
To press rewind,
Go back to a life
That I left behind.

Back to a time
When everything felt right,
I close my eyes and
Let my spirit take flight.

Back at the Start

What do you do in a world full of haters?
When your heart feels like it's got nothing but craters.

When the people you thought that you once knew,
Turn into strangers and nothing seems true.

Where do you go when it all falls apart?
When you lose everything you had
and you're back at the start.

So Many Disasters

So many disasters, and I'm sitting
here on the bathroom floor,
So many disasters, I hear dad screaming
at mum outside the door.
All the hurt and the pain,
All the lying in vain.
Bring nothing but tears and shame.

So many disasters, I can't take this shit no more,
So many disasters, I've been through all this hurt before.
They say nothing ventured nothing gained,
You try and try it's all the same.
But I feel like I'm always to blame.

Blue

I love him so
I really do,
This will grow
Like me and you.

You stole my heart,
Then tore it apart.
This too is true,
And now I'm blue.

Selfishness and Greed

I told you how I feel.
You said you felt the same,
But why are you now playing
All these silly games.

If you know how you feel
Being honest is what I need.
You made me into a fool
With your selfishness and greed.

Vow

I overcame it all for you
Just to have my world torn apart.
You impacted everything in my life,
But then left me without my heart.

I trusted you with all my thoughts,
And I never let you down,
But then one day you broke me in two.
Telling me you don't want me around.

No other heartaches can compare,
To how I feel right now,
Everything feels as broken
As the words within our vow.

I Dream

I dream of a love
So touching and so true,
I need someone to share it with
I want it to be you.

I've Been

I've been locked up by my own darkness.
I've been trapped by the things I dread.
I've been stuck inside a nightmare,
Of thoughts flooding through my head.

I've been dreaming for so long.
I've forgotten how to move.
I've tried to leave the past behind,
But there's something I must prove.

Giving up was never an option.
There is just too much at stake.
Leave all those thoughts behind me,
Now it's time for me to wake!

Sturdy Steed

There's something about you that captured my heart.
It's like I am a magnet and you are the dart.
From the moment I met you I felt a spark.
You became the light that shone through the dark.

It's like I've known you a lifetime, yet we only just met.
I have to be honest, I can't live with regret.
I've never met anyone quite like you, it's true.
I think of the life we could have and what we might do.

You unlocked my feelings that were lost in the past.
I thought they were lost forever, it's like a spell's been cast.
I'm excited for the future, and where it may lead.
You came into my life like a knight, on a sturdy steed.

Wherever the road will take us, neither of us knows.
But I'm sure whatever happens we'll continue to grow.
You are a part of my life now, almost like you always were,
And everything before you just seems like a blur.

All That I Am

For all the years I've been alive,
The Challenges faced but continued to strive.
I thank the lord for all that I am.
I know I have a purpose and I'm a part of his plan.

Sometimes I struggle this is true.
People have hurt me and made me feel blue.
Sometimes I was made to feel like I don't belong,
But I hold my head high knowing I am strong.

I am lucky in so many ways.
I have experienced many amazing days.
As I lift myself up and follow my heart,
It's never too late to make a fresh start.

If there's one thing you take from reading these pages.
Remember, life is full of journeys and stages.
Don't let the days of sorrow be your defeat.
Be kind to yourself and all others you meet.

About the Author

Fiona Porch was born and raised in Sydney, Australia and is a budding new author who has spent her life using her trials and achievements to inspire her work. Starting with singing and song writing her first album cover title song "I Am Who I Am" was inspired from her first published work, "Feelings" a poem that was printed in the NSW Department of Education and Training Resource Magazine.

Fiona has always tried to display her emotions in such a way as to help others to leap their hurdles and pursue their goals. She now invites others to share in her experiences through her literary works, hoping that her message will become a boon for all those who want to fly.

www.ingramcontent.com/pod-product-compliance
Lightning Source LLC
Chambersburg PA
CBHW032036290426
44110CB00012B/822